Seven Wonders of
THE SUN AND OTHER STARS

Rosanna Hansen

For Corwith, the supernova in my universe,
and for my dear friend Kate Melady

ACKNOWLEDGMENTS
Many thanks to the astronomers at Kitt Peak National Observatory, the Hayden
Planetarium, and Griffith Observatory for their expertise and kindness in answering my
questions and discussing how best to explain astronomy to young readers. Grateful thanks
go also to my star-gazing friends, especially Kristina Muller and John Farrell, for their love
of all things astronomical and for their friendship. In addition, I would like to thank my
wise and talented editor, Peg Goldstein, for her expert eye and incisive pen.

Twenty-First Century Books
A division of Lerner Publishing Group, Inc.
241 First Avenue North
Minneapolis, MN 55401 U.S.A.

Website address: www.lernerbooks.com

Library of Congress Cataloging-in-Publication Data

Hansen, Rosanna.
        Seven wonders of the sun and other stars / by Rosanna Hansen.
            p.   cm. — (Seven wonders)
        Includes bibliographical references and index.
        ISBN 978–0–7613–5450–5 (lib. bdg. : alk. paper)
            1. Sun—Miscellanea—Juvenile literature. 2. Supergiant stars—Juvenile literature. 3. Neutron stars—Juvenile literature.
        4. Black holes (Astronomy)—Juvenile literature. I. Title.
        QB521.5.H215 2011
        523.7—dc22   2010028448

Manufactured in the United States of America
1 – DP – 12/31/10

Contents

INTRODUCTION

$\mathcal{P}$EOPLE LOVE TO MAKE LISTS OF THE BIGGEST AND THE BEST. ALMOST TWENTY-FIVE HUNDRED YEARS AGO, A GREEK WRITER NAMED HERODOTUS MADE A LIST OF THE MOST AWESOME THINGS EVER BUILT BY PEOPLE. THE LIST INCLUDED BUILDINGS, STATUES, AND OTHER OBJECTS THAT WERE LARGE, WONDROUS, AND IMPRESSIVE. LATER, OTHER WRITERS ADDED NEW ITEMS TO THE LIST. WRITERS EVENTUALLY AGREED ON A FINAL LIST. IT WAS CALLED THE SEVEN WONDERS OF THE ANCIENT WORLD.

The list became so famous that people began imitating it. They made other lists of wonders. They listed the Seven Wonders of the Modern World and the Seven Wonders of the Middle Ages. People also made lists of wonders of science and technology.

BEYOND EARTH

But Earth is not the only place with wonders. The Sun has many wonders too. The Sun is a star. Like most stars, the Sun is a gigantic ball of hot, burning gases. The Sun's gases blaze with brilliant light. Without the Sun's light and heat, no life could exist on Earth. Our planet would be a cold, lifeless world.

The Sun is the center of our solar system. Planets, moons, and other objects in the solar system orbit, or travel around, the Sun. Smaller objects, such as comets and asteroids, orbit the Sun too. Our solar system is part of the Milky Way galaxy. A galaxy is a huge collection of stars, dust, and gas.

Up close, the Sun is a violent, stormy place. Its hot gases constantly bubble and spin. Sometimes huge explosions erupt from the Sun.

Millions of stars from the Milky Way galaxy dot the skies above Earth. Our solar system is part of this galaxy, one of billions in the universe. Find out what makes our night sky so bright—and what else might be lurking out there.

Some scientists study the Sun and its stormy weather. Scientists who study the Sun and other objects in space are called astronomers.

Far beyond the Sun and the solar system are billions and billions of other stars. For centuries, people have marveled at these faraway stars at night. What incredible wonders might these stars have to show us?

EXPLORING THE SUN AND OTHER STARS

This book explores seven wonders of the Sun and other stars. Our tour begins with the Sun, our local star. We'll learn about amazing solar flares—violent explosions on the Sun. Next, we'll watch our Moon block the Sun's light, creating an awesome solar eclipse. We'll leave the solar system to visit nebulas, where new stars are born. Next, we'll explore supergiant stars, the largest stars in the universe. We'll also visit neutron stars, the smallest and strangest stars in the universe. The last wonders on our tour are black holes. But don't get too close—you might get pulled inside and disappear. Read on to start your tour of these wonders of space.

1 SOLAR *Storms*

The Sun is the star at the center of our solar system. The Sun's powerful energy warms Earth and gives us light.

*I*N OCTOBER 2003, A HUGE SOLAR FLARE EXPLODED FROM THE SUN. ITS TONGUES OF BURNING GAS LEAPED THOUSANDS OF MILES INTO SPACE. THE FLARE'S EXPLOSION PRODUCED MORE POWER THAN TEN MILLION HYDROGEN BOMBS. IT WAS THE SUN'S MOST POWERFUL EXPLOSION IN THIRTY YEARS.

When the flare exploded, it sent an enormous cloud blasting out into space. The cloud contained billions of electrically charged particles. It also contained powerful waves of radiation, a kind of energy.

In less than a day, the cloud slammed into Earth's magnetic field. The field is a set of invisible lines around Earth where magnetism can be felt. Magnetism is a force that pulls objects together or pushes them away from one another.

This computer-generated image shows a solar flare (left) exploding out toward Earth (right). Earth's magnetic field is shown in blue. Energy from a solar flare can disturb Earth's magnetic field, disrupting electrical and communication systems on Earth.

The collision set off a big magnetic storm, a disturbance of the magnetic field. This kind of storm can hurt electrical power systems. For instance, in 1989 a magnetic storm damaged power lines in Quebec, Canada. People in some parts of Quebec had no electricity for nine hours.

Magnetic storms can cause other problems too. They can damage or disrupt radio communications, Global Positioning Systems (GPS), and cell phone service.

BRACING FOR TROUBLE

Astronomers watched closely as the huge solar flare exploded in October 2003. They tracked the flare so they could warn people about it. For instance, they told workers at power companies to prepare their equipment for a magnetic storm. With advance warning, power companies could take action to keep the electricity from going out.

Luckily, the magnetic storm was not as bad as astronomers had feared. The charged particles that caused the storm did not hit Earth's magnetic field directly. They hit at an angle, causing less damage. The storm weakened quickly. Its blast of energy soon died away. It caused only minor damage to communications systems.

But the magnetic storm also had a positive effect. It created spectacular auroras. Auroras are

AWESOME *Auroras*

Auroras are swirling curtains of colorful lights in the night sky. They are usually green but can also be red, purple, blue, or white.

Auroras occur when the solar wind carries electrically charged particles from the Sun to Earth's magnetic field. When the particles enter this field, they move toward the north and south poles. As they move, the particles rub against gases in Earth's atmosphere. The electrical charges in the particles cause the atmosphere to glow. Some auroras cover thousands of miles.

Normally, auroras appear only near the north and south poles. That's why auroras are also called northern lights and southern lights. When a solar flare causes a big magnetic storm, many more particles than normal enter Earth's magnetic field. Then people in many other places can see these beautiful colored lights.

An aurora makes a spectacular display in the sky over Portage Lake in the Chugach Mountains of Alaska. Auroras are common near the north and south poles, at the top and bottom of Earth's magnetic field. An aurora happens when particles from the Sun hit the magnetic field and cause the atmosphere to glow.

bands of glowing, colored lights in the sky. People in many parts of the world saw swirling curtains of light when the magnetic storm hit. The beauty of the shimmering, dancing lights was awe inspiring.

"When I was eight years old, I watched auroras swirling in the winter skies of Minnesota. They looked like glowing curtains of colored light. I was lucky to see them so far from the North Pole. Later on, I learned that the auroras I saw were caused by a big solar flare exploding from the Sun."

—Lee Hansen, science writer, 2008

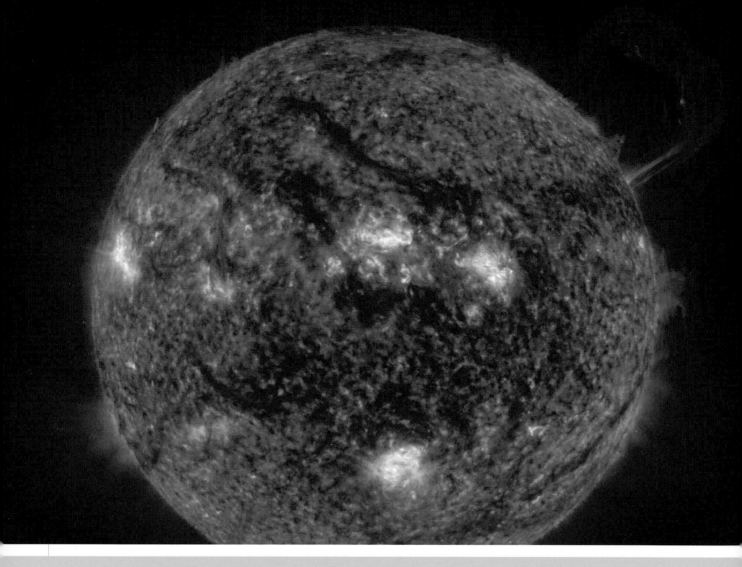

The Extreme Ultraviolet Imaging Telescope took this picture of the Sun. The telescope is on board the Solar and Heliospheric Observatory (SOHO), *a spacecraft that orbits the Sun.*

OUR AMAZING SUN

The Sun measures about 860,000 miles (1,384,000 kilometers) across. That's one hundred times wider than Earth. If the Sun were hollow, more than one million planets the size of Earth would fit inside it. The Sun is extremely heavy too. It is about six hundred times heavier than all the planets in our solar system put together.

Like most other stars, the Sun is a huge ball of hot, burning gases. The surface of the Sun burns at about 10,000°F (5,537°C). The core, or center, of the Sun is even hotter. The core burns at about 27 million°F (15 million°C).

> *"The Sun is vital to life because its light makes plants grow. When you eat a plant—a carrot, a banana, a slice of bread—you are eating the product of sunlight."*
>
> —Ken Croswell, U.S. astronomer, 2007

The Sun's core is like a giant furnace. Inside this furnace, hydrogen turns into helium. This change is called a nuclear reaction. Nuclear reactions release huge amounts of energy. The energy boils up from the core all the way to the Sun's surface.

Like Earth, the Sun has an atmosphere, a layer of gases surrounding its surface. The outermost layer of the Sun's atmosphere is called the corona, which means "crown." The corona looks a little like a halo, or crown of light, around the Sun.

From the corona, the energy created in the Sun's core flows into space. The Sun releases this energy in two main ways. First, the Sun sends out waves of radiation. These waves include the sunlight we can see and the warm rays of heat we can feel. Second, the Sun sends out tiny electrically charged particles.

The constant stream of radiation and particles from the Sun is called the solar wind. This wind from the Sun is very different from any wind on Earth. As the solar wind flows out toward Earth and far beyond, it carries the light, heat, and other energy of the Sun.

The Sun's light and heat are vitally important to our planet. Without sunlight, there would be no life on Earth. Green plants could not grow. Animals and people would have nothing to eat. And Earth itself would be a frozen, lifeless world.

SUNSPOTS

Like Earth, the Sun rotates, or spins around. The areas near the equator, the widest part of the Sun, spin faster than its north and south poles.

Also like Earth, the Sun has a magnetic field. The magnetic field is made up of invisible field lines. They run between the Sun's north and south poles. At the equator, where the Sun rotates fastest, these lines get stretched out. This stretching tangles up the magnetic field lines, like an old garden hose or a twisted computer cord.

The Sun's Magnetic Field

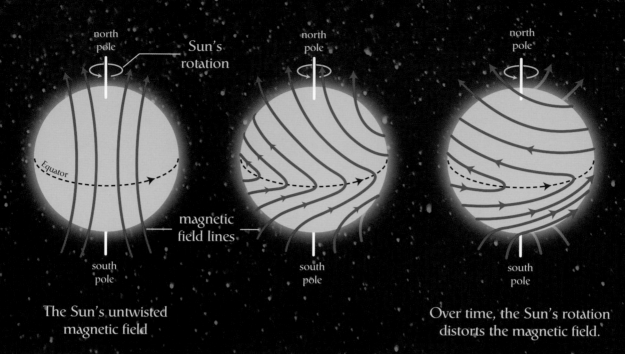

north pole

Sun's rotation

Equator

magnetic field lines

south pole

north pole

south pole

north pole

south pole

The Sun's untwisted magnetic field

Over time, the Sun's rotation distorts the magnetic field.

These tangled areas are where sunspots often occur. A sunspot is a dark, circular area on the Sun's surface. The magnetic field of a sunspot can be up to four thousand times stronger than Earth's magnetic field. The strong magnetic fields in sunspots block the burning gases rising from the Sun's core. That's why the sunspots are cooler and darker than the rest of the Sun's surface.

Solar Flares

Sunspots often appear in pairs or groups. Magnetic field lines rise up from one sunspot and loop down into another. These lines, too, can get tangled. Tension builds up and up until

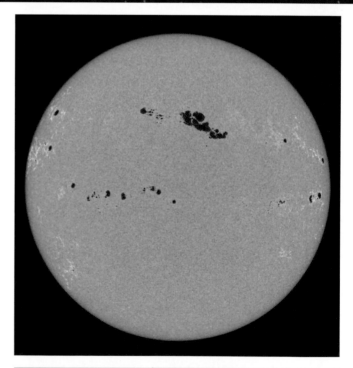

Sunspots are the black spots on this photo of the Sun. They group together along magnetic field lines.

SPOTTING *Sunspots*

An Italian astronomer named Galileo Galilei (1564–1642) studied the Sun. He used his homemade telescope to see the Sun more closely. As he watched, he noticed some dark spots on the Sun's face. Galileo had discovered sunspots!

After Galileo, no one learned much more about sunspots for hundreds of years. Then, in the early 1900s, U.S. astronomer George Ellery Hale *(below)* began studying the Sun. In 1908 Hale found that sunspots have powerful magnetic fields. His discovery was a big breakthrough for scientists. Before Hale made his discovery, people thought that only Earth had magnetic fields.

finally, something snaps. This sudden release of energy results in a huge explosion—a solar flare.

Solar flares can extend many thousands of miles into space. They can last from a few seconds to several hours. Flares release an amazing amount of energy.

Sunspots occur in twenty-two-year cycles. Each cycle starts slowly. Gradually, more and more sunspots pop up. As the cycle moves toward its peak, solar flares and other solar storms break out. The buildup reaches a peak after about eleven years. After the peak, the activity gradually slows down over another eleven years.

STORMY WEATHER ON THE SUN

Scientists call the stormy activity on the Sun its weather. When the sunspot cycle is at its height, the Sun's weather is usually most severe. Solar flares are the shortest and the most violent of any stormy weather on the Sun. But other solar storms are powerful too. Solar prominences and coronal mass ejections are two other kinds of solar storms.

A solar prominence happens when a dense tongue of gas loops out from the surface of the Sun. It arches high into the corona. Prominences

This coronal mass ejection (CME) spanned 365,400 miles (588,000 km) across the solar surface.

can be more than 100,000 miles (161,000 km) long. They can stay in place for weeks or even months.

A coronal mass ejection (CME) begins when a huge explosion in the Sun's corona sends an enormous bubble of gases ballooning out into the solar wind. A CME spews out radiation and billions of tons of electrically charged particles. CMEs can cause big magnetic storms on Earth, just like those caused by solar flares.

The radiation from a CME can hit Earth's outer atmosphere within minutes of the explosion. The radiation might disrupt radio communications on Earth. An hour or so later, the fastest of the charged particles from the CME start to arrive. As the particles get close to Earth, they can damage or destroy space satellites. (Satellites are remotely controlled spacecraft that orbit Earth. People use them to study the weather, transmit television and telephone signals, and take pictures of Earth.) The particles can also damage piloted spacecraft, such as space shuttles.

Then, a day or so after the first particles arrive, the rest of the energy from the CME smacks into Earth's atmosphere. This collision causes magnetic storms and auroras.

PREDICTING THE SUN'S STORMY WEATHER

Because solar storms can cause big problems on Earth, astronomers want to predict them accurately. To do that, astronomers study the Sun with special Earth-based telescopes. The McMath-Pierce Solar Telescope is the largest solar telescope in the world. The telescope has a tower nearly 100 feet (30 m) tall. From this tower, a shaft slants about 200 feet (60 m) to the ground. The shaft then continues underground, forming a tunnel where the Sun can be viewed. The McMath-Pierce telescope is located at Kitt Peak National Observatory in Arizona. Astronomers use this gigantic telescope to study sunspots and other stormy weather on the Sun.

But no matter how big they are, Earth-based telescopes are limited. To look at the Sun from the surface of Earth, we must look through Earth's atmosphere. That's like looking through a thick cloudy lens. For a clearer view, astronomers use telescopes on spacecraft to study the Sun. These space telescopes orbit above Earth's atmosphere.

The McMath-Pierce Solar Telescope is located at the Kitt Peak National Observatory in Arizona. Astronomers use the telescope to study the Sun's stormy weather.

SOHO, *launched in 1995, captured this image of a coronal mass ejection on April 2, 2001. The CME* (seen on the right side of the Sun in this photo) *blasted into space at approximately 4.5 million miles (7.2 million km) per hour. The solid red ring in the image is part of the photograph, not the actual Sun.*

A Closer Look

In 1995 the U.S. National Aeronautics and Space Administration (NASA) and the European Space Agency (ESA) launched the *Solar and Heliospheric Observatory* (*SOHO*). *SOHO* orbits the Sun. It has telescopes, cameras, and other instruments on board. As *SOHO* travels around the Sun, it takes one image every ten to fifteen minutes. Its instruments send images and other information back to Earth. Thanks to *SOHO*, astronomers get regular information on sunspots and bigger storms brewing on the Sun.

NASA launched two spacecraft called *STEREO* in 2006. As the two spacecraft circle the Sun, one flies in front of the other. As they fly, both spacecraft take images of the Sun at the same time, each from its own position. Astronomers combined each set of two images to make one image. Combining two images in this way forms a three-dimensional image of the Sun.

In 2010 NASA launched a spacecraft called the *Solar Dynamics Observatory* (*SDO*). *SDO* carries four telescopes and other high-tech instruments. Its telescopes take images of sunspots and other activity on the Sun's surface.

PROBING *the Sun*

In 2018 NASA is scheduled to launch the *Solar Probe Plus* spacecraft *(below)*. Smaller than a typical family car, the probe will plunge into the Sun's atmosphere. Instruments on the probe will measure, monitor, and analyze the solar wind, the Sun's magnetic field, and the Sun's energy. The probe will be able to withstand the Sun's powerful radiation and extremely high temperatures.

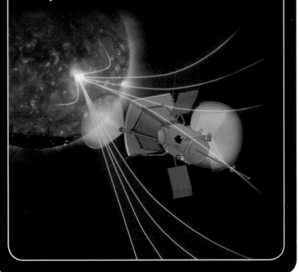

These images are ten times more detailed than the images you see on high-definition TV. Other instruments map the Sun's magnetic field and give astronomers a better understanding of violent solar storms.

Thanks to their research, astronomers can provide early and accurate warnings about solar storms. They can tell power grid operators when to expect a solar storm. They can also warn airline pilots, ship captains, and travelers about interference with GPS systems and other navigational devices. In addition, astronomers can tell satellite operators and astronauts working in space to take special precautions against upcoming storms on the Sun. And that's good news for all of us on—or near—Earth.

2 SOLAR Eclipses

The Sun disappears behind the Moon during a solar eclipse. The glowing halo of light is the Sun's corona.

IN ANCIENT CHINA, PEOPLE BELIEVED THAT A DRAGON SOMETIMES TRIED TO EAT THE SUN. IF THE SUN GREW DARK IN THE DAYTIME, PEOPLE THOUGHT THE DRAGON WAS STARTING TO GULP IT DOWN. THEY RAN OUTSIDE AND MADE LOUD NOISES TO SCARE AWAY THE DRAGON. THEY BANGED ON DRUMS, RANG GONGS, AND LIT FIRECRACKERS. THEY WERE AFRAID THE SUN WOULD DISAPPEAR FOREVER.

In modern times, we know what the ancient Chinese really saw. The sky event that frightened them was not caused by a dragon. Instead, the Moon had blocked out the light of the Sun. When the Moon blocks the Sun's light, the sky gets dark in daytime. Scientists call this event an eclipse of the Sun, or solar eclipse. (*Eclipse* means "to block out.")

Townspeople observe a solar eclipse in this painting by French artist Antoine Caron (1521–1599). In Caron's day, astronomers did not know much about the movements of Earth, the Sun, and the Moon. Some people worried that the Sun would disappear forever during an eclipse.

This solar eclipse took place on January 15, 2010. In time-lapse photography, it is possible to see (from left to right) *how the Moon passes in front of the Sun, blocking it out in the center part of the image.*

The Moon orbits, or travels around, Earth about once a month. As the Moon orbits Earth, it casts a shadow. A solar eclipse happens when the Moon moves between the Sun and Earth. When the Sun, the Moon, and Earth all line up in a straight line, the Moon can block out the light of the Sun, which casts a shadow on Earth. The result? An awesome solar eclipse. From two to five times a year, the Moon's shadow falls directly on Earth, causing an eclipse. The rest of the time, the shadow of the Moon falls either below or above Earth—not on it.

IN THE SHADOW OF THE MOON

During an eclipse, the Moon's shadow sweeps rapidly across Earth. The Moon moves at a speed of about 2,000 miles (3,200 km) per hour.

A FORCE CALLED *Gravity*

What makes the Moon circle around Earth? What makes Earth and the other planets circle around the Sun? The Moon travels around Earth and the planets travel around the Sun because of gravity.

Every object in our solar system has gravity. Everything pulls at everything else. The more mass, or matter, an object has, the more gravity it has. The more gravity an object has, the harder it can pull at other things.

The Sun is by far the biggest object in our solar system. So the Sun has the strongest gravity and the strongest pull. Its gravity pulls at the planets and keeps them circling in their orbits.

COVER Up

When viewed from Earth, the Sun appears to be about the same size as the Moon. In reality, the Sun is four hundred times wider than the Moon. So why do the Sun and the Moon look about the same size in the sky? How can the tiny Moon block the light from the gigantic Sun during a total eclipse? The answer is distance. The Moon is about four hundred times closer to Earth than the Sun is. Objects that are closer to us look bigger than those far away. During a total eclipse, with the Moon and the Sun lined up, the Moon appears to cover the Sun completely.

As the moon moves, its shadow travels with it. The dark center of the shadow makes a narrow path as it travels across Earth. This narrow center is called the eclipse path, or umbra. People in the path of the dark umbra will see a total eclipse. During the time the eclipse is total, the Sun will be completely blocked out by the Moon.

Surrounding the dark umbra of the Moon's shadow is a lighter, wider area called the penumbra. People in the path of the penumbra will see a partial eclipse of the Sun. During a partial eclipse, the Moon blocks out only some of the Sun.

A SOLAR ECLIPSE

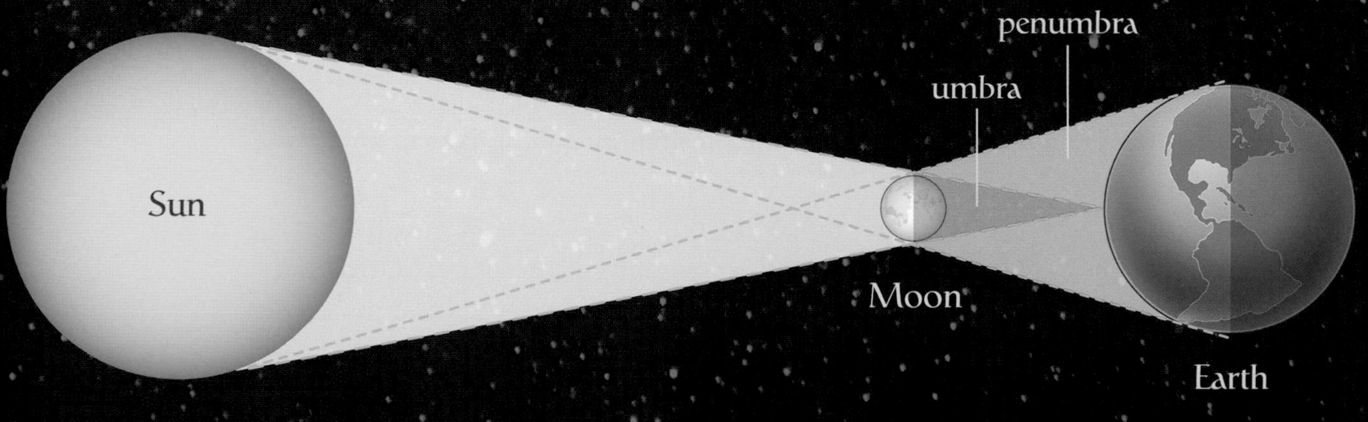

Sun

Moon

penumbra

umbra

Earth

Sometimes a ring-shaped, or annular, eclipse takes place. This type of eclipse occurs when the Moon is at its farthest point from Earth. At this time, the Moon blocks only the middle part of the Sun. People in the path of the annular eclipse can see a bright ring of the Sun surrounding the dark disk of the Moon.

VIEWING A TOTAL ECLIPSE

A total solar eclipse is one of the strangest, most wonderful sights in the world. Some people travel thousands of miles to see a total eclipse in person.

Imagine you are in the right spot to see a total eclipse. First, you will see the Moon move toward the Sun's western edge. When the Moon reaches the Sun, a little nick of darkness will appear on the side of the Sun. Slowly, the Moon will slide over more and more of the Sun. After about thirty minutes, the Sun will be more than half covered.

As the Moon moves farther, the sky will darken. It will turn silvery gray. Slowly, the remaining sunshine will shrink down to only a few bright dots of light. At last only one bright dot will remain. Then the dot will fade. The Sun will be completely hidden by the black disk of the Moon. The sky will grow eerily dark. The eclipse will be total. Astronomers call this part of an eclipse the totality.

Around the black disk of the Moon, you will still see a glowing halo of white light. This halo is the corona, the outer atmosphere of the Sun. It is visible because its feathery gases stream out far into space. Beyond the corona, you may see a few stars and planets in the dark sky.

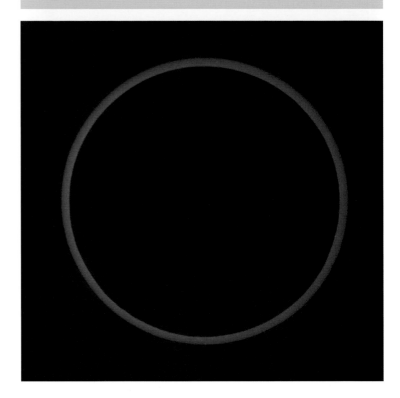

This photograph shows an annular eclipse of the Sun. During an annular eclipse, the Moon covers up only the center of the Sun. A bright ring of sunlight behind the Moon is still visible.

ECLIPSE *Calendar*

Astronomers know the orbits of the Moon and Earth in space. They know exactly when the Sun, the Moon, and Earth will line up to create an eclipse. This chart shows where total and annular eclipses will occur from 2012 to 2020.

Sometimes an eclipse is total for some of its path over Earth and then annular for another part of its path. This situation is shown on the chart as a mixed, or hybrid, eclipse.

DATE	AREA OF VISIBILITY	ECLIPSE TYPE
May 20, 2012	China, Japan, Pacific Ocean, western United States	annular
November 13, 2012	northern Australia, South Pacific Ocean	total
May 10, 2013	northern Australia, Solomon Islands, central Pacific Ocean	annular
November 3, 2013	Atlantic Ocean, central Africa	hybrid
April 29, 2014	Antarctica	annular
March 20, 2015	North Atlantic Ocean, Faroe Islands	total
March 9, 2016	Indonesia, Pacific Ocean	total
September 1, 2016	Atlantic Ocean, central Africa, Madagascar, Indian Ocean	annular
February 26, 2017	Pacific, Chile, Argentina, Atlantic Ocean, Africa	annular
August 21, 2017	northern Pacific Ocean, parts of the United States (Oregon, Idaho, Wyoming, Nebraska, Missouri, Illinois, Kentucky, Tennessee, North Carolina, South Carolina), South Atlantic Ocean	total
July 2, 2019	South Pacific Ocean, Chile, Argentina	total
December 26, 2019	Saudi Arabia, India, Indonesia	annular
June 21, 2020	central Africa, southern Asia, China, Pacific Ocean	annular
December 14, 2020	South Pacific Ocean, Chile, Argentina, South Atlantic Ocean	total

Above: *A photographer captured these images of a total eclipse of the Sun in Libya in 2006.*
Below: *Observers of a 2009 solar eclipse in China wear special glasses to protect their eyes.*

Hello, *Helium*

One day in 1868, British astronomer Joseph Norman Lockyer *(below)* was watching a total eclipse of the Sun. While he watched, he made scientific observations. Through his observations, he identified a new gas in an outer layer of the Sun. Lockyer named the gas helium, after the Greek word *helios*, or Sun. Twenty-seven years later, scientists discovered helium on Earth.

DURING THE DARKNESS

During the darkness of a total eclipse, birds and other animals get confused. The birds fly home to roost, just as they would at night. Cows stop eating and head for the barn. Horses may stop in their tracks and refuse to move.

The period of totality, during which the Moon completely covers the Sun, can last for seven and a half minutes but is often much briefer. After this period, a dot of light appears. Next, a sliver of the Sun can be seen once more. The darkness begins to lift as the Moon moves slowly away from the Sun. Gradually, the daylight returns to normal.

HOW TO WATCH AN ECLIPSE

If you have a chance to watch an eclipse in person, you must protect your eyes. The Sun's powerful light can badly damage your eyes during an eclipse. You can buy special glasses or filters to watch an eclipse. Be sure the equipment is rated safe for eclipse viewing.

"Of all the events in nature that can be predicted . . . the most awesome is a total eclipse of the Sun."
—*Fred Schaaf, U.S. astronomer, 2007*

ECLIPSE MYTHS AND LEGENDS

Eclipses have inspired myths and legends since ancient times. In some ancient cultures, people feared the Sun was bewitched during an eclipse. They thought it was going to die. The Mayan people of Central America tried to save the Sun with special ceremonies. People in ancient Europe made lots of noise to protect the Sun from demons.

People in ancient Scandinavia told myths to explain solar eclipses. They said that a wolflike giant followed the Sun and tried to devour it. An Egyptian myth said that an evil black pig leaped into the eye of Horus, the sky god, and blocked the Sun's light.

SOLAR ECLIPSE *Viewer*

One safe way to view a solar eclipse is to watch it indirectly with a pinhole projector. You can make a pinhole projector with a cardboard box. Place a piece of white paper inside one end of the box. On the opposite end, cut a small square hole. Cover the hole with aluminum foil. Make a tiny hole in the aluminum foil with a pin. Put the box over your head with your back to the Sun. Look at the white paper inside the box. The light shining through the pinhole will form an image of the eclipse on the white paper. You can use your pinhole projector to watch the entire eclipse taking place behind you.

BUILD YOUR OWN SOLAR ECLIPSE VIEWER

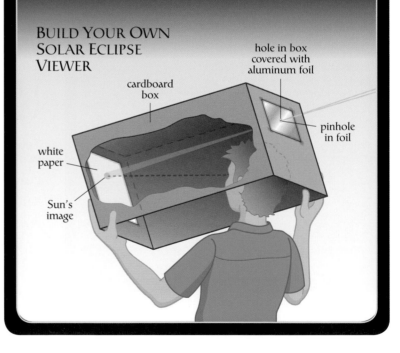

hole in box covered with aluminum foil

cardboard box

pinhole in foil

white paper

Sun's image

"A total eclipse . . . is a sight that well repays an observer for his effort in traveling to the zone of totality. In any given location a total eclipse can be seen, on the average, only once in 360 years."

—Fred Whipple, U.S. astronomer, 1981

3 Nebulas

Inside the Orion Nebula, gases and dust clump together and heat up. Eventually, the gases get hot enough to form stars.

$\mathcal{A}$BOUT ONE MILLION YEARS AGO, A BRAND-NEW STAR BEGAN TO SHINE FOR THE FIRST TIME. THE BRIGHT YOUNG STAR WAS WRAPPED IN A HUGE CLOUD OF DUST AND GAS. ENORMOUS CLOUDS OF GAS AND DUST IN SPACE ARE CALLED NEBULAS. NEBULAS ARE THE NURSERIES WHERE NEW STARS BEGIN TO FORM. THE BRAND-NEW STAR FORMED IN THE ORION NEBULA, THE NEBULA CLOSEST TO EARTH. THE ORION NEBULA IS THE BIRTHPLACE OF MANY NEW STARS.

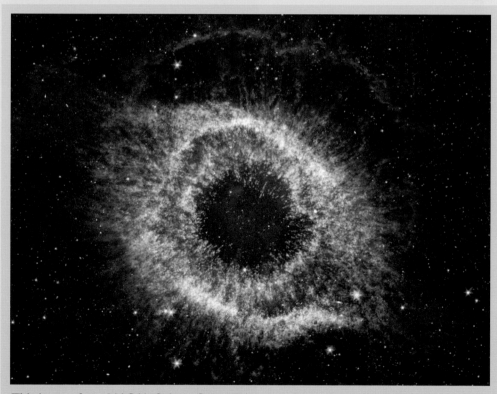

This image from NASA's Spitzer Space Telescope shows the Helix Nebula in the constellation Aquarius. The nebula looks like a human eyeball.

BIG AND BEAUTIFUL

Nebulas are some of the most wonderful sights in the universe. They glow with beautiful colors and take interesting shapes. The Cone Nebula looks like a huge, fluffy pillar. The Lagoon Nebula looks like a swirling pond or lagoon. The Horsehead Nebula looks a little like the knight in a chess set.

Some nebulas glow from the heat of the young stars inside them. Other nebulas are dark. Still other nebulas are lit up by stars shining near them.

The Orion Nebula is the easiest one to find in the night sky. It is in the constellation Orion. A constellation is a shape formed by stars in the sky. The constellation Orion looks like a giant hunter. He has a sword hanging below his belt. The Orion Nebula is in the middle of his sword.

People can see this nebula with just their eyes. The nebula looks like a misty gray cloud. But a telescope shows much more color and detail. With powerful telescopes, astronomers can see thousands of newborn stars glowing inside the nebula. The new stars look like red dots with white-hot blazing centers. Wrapped around the baby stars are the nebula's dusty clouds of glowing gas. The clouds glow with red, white, and other colors.

SHAPES IN *the Sky*

People first started naming constellations in ancient times. They thought groups of stars looked like animals, gods, people, and objects. People named constellations after the shapes they saw. For instance, the constellation Cassiopeia is named for a character in Greek mythology. Orion the Hunter, who has both a constellation and a nebula named for him, is also a character from Greek mythology. The constellation Lupus looks like a wolf. *Lupus* means "wolf" in Latin. The constellation Cygnus looks like a swan, and the name means "swan" in Latin. The constellation Scorpius looks like a scorpion.

CONSTELLATION ORION

Betelgeuse

Orion Nebula

Rigel

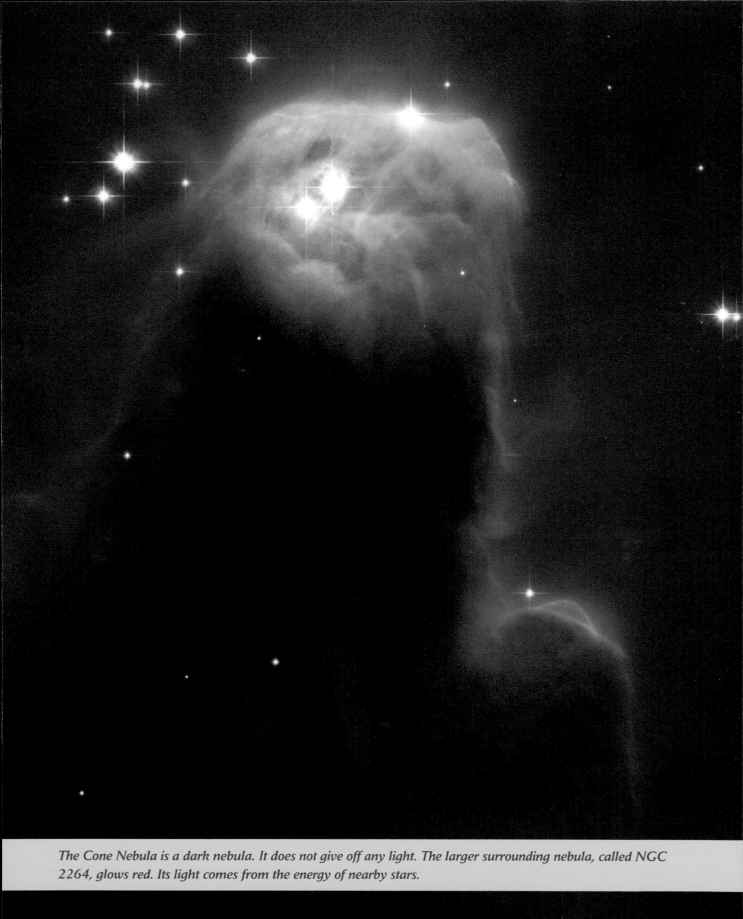

The Cone Nebula is a dark nebula. It does not give off any light. The larger surrounding nebula, called NGC 2264, glows red. Its light comes from the energy of nearby stars.

Left: *The dark, mysterious Horsehead Nebula offers views of new stars being born in a shroud of dark dust and gases.*

Below: *French astronomer Guillaume Le Gentil discovered the Lagoon Nebula in 1747. People who live in the Northern Hemisphere (the northern half of Earth) can see the nebula without a telescope, although it looks very faint.*

BIRTHPLACE OF THE STARS

Nebulas are clouds, but they are different from our clouds on Earth. Our clouds are filled with tiny ice crystals and water droplets. A nebula is filled with particles of gas and dust. Most of the gas is hydrogen. The rest of the gas is helium.

Sometimes the particles of gas and dust in a nebula bump into one another. Gradually, some of the particles start to clump together. Over millions of years, the clumps of gas and dust get bigger. As they get bigger, gravity pulls the clumps more and more tightly together. The tighter the clumps, the hotter they become. After millions of years, the gas in the clumps gets incredibly hot.

When the gas gets hot enough, the blazing heat sets off a nuclear reaction. In this reaction, hydrogen changes into helium. The reaction blasts out huge amounts of energy, like a giant hydrogen bomb. At that moment, the new star begins to shine.

LOOKING INSIDE NEBULAS

When a star first starts to shine, it is still wrapped in the nebula that gave it birth. This dusty cloud blocks the light shining from the baby star. But the light from the star heats up the nebula. The nebula gives off infrared radiation.

Infrared radiation is an invisible kind of energy. Our eyes can't see infrared radiation, but our bodies can feel its heat. Astronomers use special infrared telescopes to look through nebulas. With these telescopes, astronomers can detect heat waves from the warm dust and hot new stars inside nebulas. They can "see" deep inside nebulas and learn their secrets.

"Stars progress from a cloudy birth in a dark pocket of interstellar hydrogen gas to a glorious death in a fantastic celestial [heavenly] light show."

—*Mark Voit, U.S. astronomer, 2000*

> *"For a moment of night we have a glimpse of ourselves and of our world islanded in its stream of stars . . . voyaging between horizons across the eternal seas of space and time."*
>
> —*Henry Beston, U.S. author, describing stars, 1928*

The Spitzer Space Telescope is the largest infrared telescope ever built. NASA launched the Spitzer into orbit in 2003. From its orbit in space, the Spitzer probes the mysteries of distant nebulas. The telescope has shown us amazing sights, including star-forming nebulas, brand-new stars, and other secrets of the nebulas.

PLANETARY NEBULAS

Some of the most beautiful nebulas are called planetary nebulas. These nebulas have spectacular rings of different colors. They form when a star called a red giant gets old and dies. As it dies, the red giant star puffs its outer layers of gas out into space. Only the dead core of the star is left behind. The outer layers of gas form an enormous ring around the dead core of the star.

The word *planetary* means "of or relating to a planet." But planetary nebulas have nothing to do with any kind of planet. The confusion started in the 1700s. Back then, a British astronomer named William Herschel studied these nebulas. Herschel's telescope was not very strong. It did not enlarge images the way powerful modern telescopes do. All Herschel could see was that the nebulas looked round, like planets. So he named these objects planetary nebulas.

In the twenty-first century, powerful telescopes reveal the true nature of planetary nebulas. With these telescopes, we can see their beautiful colors and dramatic shapes. We can also see the dead core of the star at the center of each nebula.

READY FOR ITS *Close-up*

In 1880 U.S. astronomer Henry Draper took the first photo of a nebula. He chose the Orion Nebula. This beautiful nebula is one of the brightest in the night sky. Twelve years later, Draper took an even better photo of this nebula. Since then many other people have photographed the Orion Nebula.

This planetary nebula, NGC 6302, is also known as a butterfly nebula. Can you tell why?

4 Supergiant STARS

The bright, reddish star Betelgeuse shines in the night sky.

SUPERGIANT STARS ARE THE LARGEST STARS IN THE UNIVERSE. THEY ARE ENORMOUS. ONE OF THE MOST FAMOUS SUPERGIANT STARS IS NAMED BETELGEUSE. THIS IMMENSE RED STAR ACTUALLY VARIES IN SIZE. FOR A WHILE IT, GROWS BIGGER. THEN IT SHRINKS AGAIN. AT ITS LARGEST, BETELGEUSE IS ABOUT SIX HUNDRED TIMES WIDER ACROSS THAN THE SUN.

Rigel is a blue supergiant star that is located in the Witch Head Nebula. Rigel is the sixth brightest star in the night sky.

Betelgeuse is also much brighter than the Sun. In fact, it sometimes shines fourteen thousand times brighter. Betelgeuse changes in brightness when it shrinks and grows. When it shrinks, it gets dimmer. When it expands, it brightens up again. Its light is a beautiful red-orange color.

Betelgeuse varies in size and brightness because it is an old star. It has used up most of its fuel. Growing and shrinking again is part of the aging process for supergiant stars.

MEET THE MASSIVE STARS

The Sun is a medium-sized star. Other stars are much smaller than the Sun. The biggest stars often have much more mass, or material, than other stars. That's why we call them massive stars. Massive stars are usually at least ten times wider than the Sun. They shine from one thousand to one million times more brightly than the Sun.

COLORFUL *Stars*

If you look at the stars at night, you might notice that some of them are different colors *(below)*. With a telescope, you can see their colors even better. The hottest stars are bluish white. Yellow stars are medium in heat. Red stars are the coolest.

To see how different colors indicate different temperatures, look at the flames in a fireplace. The red flames are the coolest. The yellow flames are hotter. The flame of a welder's torch is much hotter than a fire in a fireplace. It burns bluish white.

"The galaxy is nothing more but a mass of innumerable stars planted together in clusters. Upon whatever part of it you direct the telescope, straightway a vast crowd of stars presents itself to view."

—Galileo Galilei, Italian astronomer, 1610

Like all stars, massive stars are born inside nebulas. For about five million years, a massive star burns its hydrogen fuel. It shines brightly. The massive star is very hot. Its surface temperature can reach 12,000°F (6,650°C). A star's color depends on its heat. The hottest supergiants are bluish white.

The supergiant Deneb shines bluish white. When it cools down, it will turn red.

DEATH OF A SUPERSTAR

As it shines, a supergiant star burns up its hydrogen fuel. Eventually, its fuel supply grows low. When this happens, the star's outer layers swell up. At the same time, the star starts to cool off. As the star cools down, its color changes from bluish white to red. The star becomes a red supergiant.

After a while, the supergiant star runs out of hydrogen completely. When that happens, the star begins burning its helium. Then the helium runs out. So the star burns some heavier materials left in its core. Finally, the core of the star fills up with iron. The star cannot use iron as fuel and can no longer burn.

The brightest star in the constellation Scorpius is the red supergiant Antares (upper center). *The red clusters in this photograph are nebulas.*

How Far Are the Stars?

The star closest to Earth is the Sun. It is a medium-sized star, but it looks much bigger and brighter than any other star. That's because it is so much closer to us than other stars. The Sun is about 93 million miles (150 million km) from Earth.

After the Sun, the star nearest Earth is Alpha Centauri. This star is about 25 trillion miles (40 trillion km) away from Earth. Other stars are much, much farther away than Alpha Centauri. Some are millions of trillions of miles away. That's why most stars look like little, twinkling lights. They look small because they are so incredibly far away.

Scientists measure the vast distance between stars and other objects in space with a unit called a light-year. One light-year is the distance light travels in a year. That's about 5.88 trillion miles (9.46 trillion km). Alpha Centauri's distance from Earth, about 25 trillion miles (40 trillion km), equals about 4.3 light-years. That means the light leaving Alpha Centauri takes about 4.3 years to reach us here on Earth. When you look at Alpha Centauri from Earth, you are seeing light that left this star about 4.3 years ago.

Betelgeuse is about 640 light-years from Earth. If you look at Betelgeuse in the sky tonight, you will see light that left this star about 640 years ago. If Betelgeuse blows up in a supernova tomorrow, people on Earth will not see the light of its explosion for 640 years in the future.

A massive star goes out with a bang. The instant the star runs out of fuel, it is crushed by its own gravity. Its core collapses into a tiny ball. That same second, the rest of the star explodes in a spectacular blast. The explosion is called a supernova. This blast blows most of the star apart. It throws bits of matter far into space. Only the tiny core may be left behind.

Betelgeuse: Running Out of Juice

Betelgeuse is an old supergiant. It has already used up most of its fuel. When the fuel is gone, the star will explode in an astounding supernova. For about a week, the supernova's explosion will blaze as brightly as ten billion Suns. In fact, this supernova will be one of the brightest stars in the sky. Then, over several months, the supernova's brightness will slowly begin to fade.

Scientists aren't sure when Betelgeuse will explode. It might explode in a few months or in a million years.

WHERE TO SEE THE SUPERSTARS

Because supergiants are big and bright, it's easy to find them in the night sky. You can find the supergiant Antares in the constellation Scorpius. You can find the supergiant Deneb in the constellation Cygnus.

Betelgeuse and another supergiant, Rigel, are seen in the constellation Orion. Betelgeuse sits at Orion's shoulder or armpit. Rigel sits in Orion's left knee. Orion is the brightest constellation in the sky during the winter in the Northern Hemisphere, or the northern half of Earth. The stars in Orion form a picture of a giant hunter holding a club. The giant also has a sword hanging from his belt. Betelgeuse and Rigel are the two brightest stars in Orion. Together, they help make this constellation easy to find. (See the illustration on page 30.)

Mu Cephei, in the constellation Cepheus, is one of the largest supergiant stars. Astronomers also call it the Garnet Star because of its beautiful deep red color. A garnet is a dark red gemstone.

BETELGEUSE OR *Beetle Juice?*

Betelgeuse might seem like a strange name for a star. People pronounce it either BEET-ehl-joos or BEHT-ehl-jooz. The name comes from the ancient Arabic language. Experts disagree about what the name means. Some scholars think *Betelgeuse* means "armpit of the giant" in ancient Arabic. That translation makes sense, since Betelgeuse is found at the armpit of the constellation Orion, the giant hunter.

"How can Antares and Betelgeuse shine so brightly? There's only one way. These stars must be big. Really big. Really, really big—so big that astronomers call them supergiants."

—*Ken Croswell, U.S. astronomer, 2009*

Seven Wonders of the Sun and Other Stars

42

The Hubble Space Telescope *took this image of the red supergiant star V838 Monocerotis lighting up the surrounding dust and gases.*

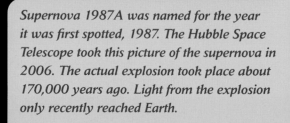

Supernova 1987A was named for the year
it was first spotted, 1987. The Hubble Space
Telescope took this picture of the supernova in
2006. The actual explosion took place about
170,000 years ago. Light from the explosion
only recently reached Earth.

$\mathcal{A}$BOUT 170,000 YEARS AGO, A SUPERGIANT

STAR EXPLODED IN ANOTHER GALAXY. THE SPECTACULAR EXPLOSION

BLEW MOST OF THE STAR APART. BITS OF THE STAR FLEW OUTWARD.

THEY TRAVELED MILLIONS OF MILES PER HOUR.

The star's explosion gave off a gigantic burst of light and other energy. The light streamed outward toward our own galaxy, the Milky Way. The light traveled about 5.88 trillion miles (9.46 trillion km) per year. In February 1987, some of the light from the exploding super star finally reached Earth.

The Kueyen Very Large Telescope took this picture of spiral galaxy NGC 1559 in 2005. The picture shows a supernova (an exploding supergiant star)—the bright, starlike dot just above the galaxy.

Canadian astronomer Ian Shelton was the first person to identify the exploding star. He had been taking photos with a camera attached to a telescope. He took some photos of the Large Magellanic Cloud (LMC), the galaxy where the supergiant star had exploded. Shelton looked at one of his photos of the LMC. He noticed a very bright star in the photo. He was puzzled. The bright star hadn't been there the night before. What had happened?

Shelton stepped outside to see the sky with his own eyes. Sure enough, he could see the bright new star. He had made a wonderful discovery. He was the first person in more than four hundred years to see the light of a supernova— an exploding supergiant star. Astronomers call this kind of explosion a Type II supernova.

BRIGHT LIGHTS

When small or medium-sized stars explode, the explosions are very bright. In earlier centuries, people thought the explosions looked like shiny new stars in the sky. In 1572

GAZILLIONS of Galaxies

A galaxy is a huge collection of stars, dust, and gas held together by gravity. One galaxy might contain billions of stars. Our own galaxy, the Milky Way, contains more than one hundred billion stars. The Milky Way is only one of many billions of galaxies in the universe. No one knows for sure how many galaxies there are. Most astronomers think the universe has at least one hundred billion galaxies.

The Milky Way is shaped like a gigantic spiral or pinwheel. It has long curving arms that sweep out from its dense, glowing center. Other galaxies have an elliptical, or egglike, shape. Still other galaxies don't have a standard shape. Astronomers call them irregular galaxies.

The billions of galaxies in the universe are not neatly placed in space. They clump together into clusters that may contain thousands of galaxies or more. Gradually, the clusters of galaxies group into superclusters. Then sometimes the superclusters are pulled closer together by gravity. As they draw nearer, they pull hard at one another. They may pull each other out of shape or even bang into one another. During these collisions of superclusters, large galaxies may even swallow smaller ones.

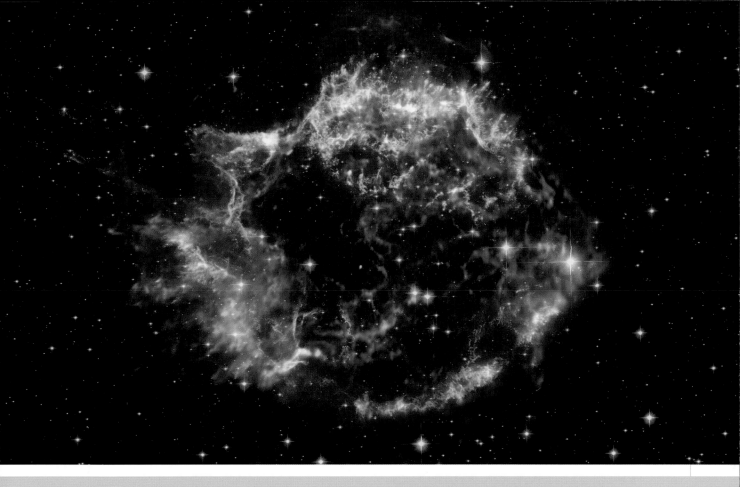

This picture shows Cassiopeia A, the remains of a supernova that appeared in the sky more than three hundred years ago. The blue wispy arches show gases that are still drifting out into space after the explosion. The red and green portions are the remains of the star that exploded.

Danish astronomer Tycho Brahe saw an exploding star in the constellation Cassiopeia. Brahe called the explosion a *nova stella,* or "new star." After that, exploding stars were called novas.

Astronomers think that twenty-five to fifty novas occur in our galaxy every year. For a few weeks, a nova may shine as brightly as one hundred thousand Suns. That's a big explosion. But when supergiants explode, they can shine millions of times brighter than the Sun. That's why an exploding supergiant is called a supernova.

"I was contemplating the stars when I noticed a new star; surpassing all the others in brilliancy, shining directly above my head. I was so astonished at the sight I doubted my own eyes."

—*Tycho Brahe, Danish astronomer, describing a supernova, 1572*

"While some stars meet their end relatively gently, others go out with a bang. The bang is known as a supernova and is one of the most dramatic events in the universe."

—Gabrielle Walker, British science writer, 1998

The supernova that Ian Shelton discovered is named Supernova 1987A, because he spotted it in 1987. Supernova 1987A was very, very bright. When Shelton first saw it, the explosion shone more brightly than one hundred million stars the size of the Sun. In a few hours, it grew even brighter. Soon it shone two hundred million times more brightly than the Sun.

Supernova 1987A shone very brightly for about three months. Then it gradually began to fade. Since then, most of Supernova 1987A has become an enormous cloud of exploded gases. These gases are still expanding outward.

THE STARS INSIDE US

When huge stars explode in supernovas, they release substances into space. These substances include iron, oxygen, and calcium. Without supernovas, these substances might stay locked inside stars forever. But once they are blasted out into space, these substances become the building blocks of life in the universe. In fact, you are made of substances that were once inside stars. Carbon, iron, calcium, and other substances are the building blocks of your body.

How did these substances from a star become part of your body? It took a very long time. First, supergiant stars exploded. These supernova explosions released dust, gas, and other substances such as carbon, iron, and calcium into space. Some of the dust, gas, and other substances eventually combined to become the planets in our solar system.

After billions of years, life began on our planet, Earth. The tiny life-forms were made of carbon, iron, and other substances thrown out from supernovas. Over billions of years more, these tiny life-forms slowly evolved, or changed. They became more and more complicated. Finally, some of the life-forms evolved into human beings. That means that humans and all other forms of life

This mass of gas and dust is all that remains of the supernova N 63A. The supernova remnant is part of a star-forming region in the Large Magellanic Cloud (LMC), an irregular galaxy 160,000 light-years from our own Milky Way galaxy and visible from the Southern Hemisphere.

on Earth are made up of substances that were once inside stars. These substances include the iron and oxygen in our blood and the calcium in our bones.

TYPE 1A SUPERNOVAS

Sometimes a supernova involves two stars, not just one. One of the stars must be a white dwarf. White dwarfs are tiny and dense. They have extremely strong gravity. The other star must be much bigger than the white dwarf.

Sirius (above) *is a white dwarf in the constellation Canis Major. Sirius is the brightest star in the night sky.*

The two stars circle one another. Their gravity holds them close together. The strong gravity of the white dwarf might start pulling gases away from the big neighboring star. The gases swirl out of the big star and into the white dwarf. As the gases move, the white dwarf gets bigger. As the dwarf gets bigger, its temperature

WHAT'S A *White Dwarf?*

A white dwarf is a tiny, hot star. A white dwarf forms when a small or medium-sized star burns up all its fuel. The star's outer layers explode. Its core starts collapsing. The core becomes the size of a small planet.

The material inside a white dwarf is packed very tightly together. That makes the star dense and heavy for its small size. A pencil box full of material from a white dwarf would weigh more than a school bus full of kids on Earth.

The Sun is a medium-sized star. When it uses up all its fuel, the Sun will become a white dwarf. Astronomers believe the Sun's fuel will last for about five billion more years. So we don't have to worry about the Sun using up its fuel in our lifetimes.

rises higher and higher. In addition, the dwarf's strong gravity squeezes its gases more and more tightly together.

Finally, the white dwarf gets so big and heavy that it can't support itself. It collapses completely. What happens then? Boom! The dwarf explodes in a supernova. The mighty blast almost blows the dwarf apart. Some of its companion star may be blown away too. An immense cloud of gases forms.

This illustration shows a white dwarf surrounded by a disk of swirling gases. The white dwarf's powerful gravity has pulled these gases away from a nearby star.

Gigantic amounts of light and other forms of energy erupt into space. This kind of supernova is called a Type 1a supernova.

SPOTTING SUPERNOVAS

In A.D. 1006, a bright star suddenly appeared in the constellation Lupus. People in Egypt, Europe, Japan, and China saw the new star. In modern times, we know this "new star" was really a supernova. It was one of the brightest ever seen. People spotted other supernovas in 1054, 1572, 1604, and 1680.

In earlier times, people usually found supernovas by accident, such as when Ian Shelton found one in his photograph. In the twenty-first century, astronomers go looking for supernovas. They use telescopes and computers to scan hundreds of distant galaxies at a time. By scanning so many galaxies, astronomers can sometimes find several supernovas in one night.

TYCHO'S *Supernova*

The exploding star that Tycho Brahe *(below)* called a new star (nova stella in Latin) was actually a supernova. As Brahe watched, the supernova blazed as brightly as the planet Venus. Then, over the next six months, its brightness slowly faded. Brahe kept careful records of changes in the supernova's brightness. Based on these records, modern astronomers believe that Brahe saw a Type 1a supernova. Astronomers still study the gas cloud that this supernova left behind.

A combined image of photos taken from the Hubble Space Telescope, Spitzer Space Telescope, and Chandra X-ray Observatory show supernova N49, the brightest supernova remnant in the Large Magellanic Cloud.

6 Neutron Stars

Inside the Crab Nebula, shown
here, is a pulsar, a neutron star that
sends out regular signals.

$\mathcal{I}$N 1054 ASTRONOMERS IN CHINA SAW A HUGE SUPERNOVA IN THE SKY. THEY CALLED THIS SUPERNOVA A GUEST STAR. THEY GAZED AT IT IN WONDER. THE SUPERNOVA BLAZED SO BRIGHTLY THAT PEOPLE COULD SEE IT EVEN IN DAYTIME. AFTER A YEAR, THE SUPERNOVA GREW DIMMER. WE CAN STILL SEE THE REMAINS OF THIS SUPERNOVA IN THE TWENTY-FIRST CENTURY. THE GAS AND DUST LEFT OVER FROM THE EXPLOSION ARE CALLED THE CRAB NEBULA.

When the supergiant star that created the supernova first exploded, its outer layers blew far out into space. But the iron core of the star did not explode. Instead, the star's huge gravity crushed the core down into a tiny ball. Gravity squeezed the particles in the ball tightly. Because the particles were so tightly packed, the core became incredibly dense. It became a tiny, dense ball called a neutron star. This star remains inside the Crab Nebula.

This illustration shows a neutron star. Neutron stars are tiny—but very dense. A neutron star 12 miles (19 km) across weighs twice as much as the Sun.

This illustration shows a neutron star with its magnetic field lines. Strong magnetic fields around neutron stars create tremendous amounts of energy.

> *"A teaspoon of material from a neutron star would weigh more than a pile of a billion cars."*
>
> —Ellen Jackson, U.S. science writer, 2008

THE DENSEST STARS

Neutron stars are very tiny compared to other stars. But they are the densest stars in the universe. They are denser than white dwarfs. They are so dense that a neutron star the size of a raindrop could weigh 1 billion tons (0.9 billion metric tons). A neutron star the size of a dime would weigh more than Mount Everest—Earth's tallest mountain. If a small piece of a neutron star were to fall on Earth, it would drill right through the middle of our planet and come out the other side. It would slice right through Earth.

A neutron star has a crust, or outer layer, made of solid iron. Beneath this iron crust is a liquid. The liquid is made of small, tightly packed particles called neutrons. These particles are tiny but are very dense. They give the neutron star its name.

A typical neutron star is only about 13 miles (20 km) across. A star that small could probably fit inside your town. Despite its small size, a neutron star has more mass than the Sun. It has three hundred thousand times more mass than Earth. Because it has so much mass, a neutron star has an enormous amount of gravity. If the star were in your town, its gravity would pull at everything in town and everything in the rest of the world. The gravity would crush our entire planet down into a teeny speck—too small to be seen without a microscope.

Some neutron stars circle around ordinary stars. The neutron stars' huge gravitational pull tugs at the neighboring stars. The neutron stars pull so hard that they suck material out of the other stars. Gradually, the neutron stars pull all the material out of ordinary stars and consume them completely. These neutron stars are a little like vampires, sucking the life from other stars.

RRAT: A New Kind of Star

In 2006 astronomers discovered a new type of neutron star. They named it a rotating radio transient, or RRAT for short. This kind of star sends out strong, quick blasts of radio waves. The blasts might happen every few minutes or every few hours. In between these bursts, the star is silent.

> *"Poets might say that the stars are forever, but scientists know that's not true. All stars eventually die when they run out of fuel."*
>
> —Science writer David Aguilar, 2007

PULSARS: STARS THAT SIGNAL

When a neutron star first forms, it spins extremely quickly. Some neutron stars spin almost one thousand times a second. But gradually, over millions of years, the spinning slows down a little.

Some neutron stars give off a narrow stream of energy while they spin. The energy is like a beam of light from a lighthouse. Inside the lighthouse, a lamp moves in a circle. As the beam of light from the lamp sweeps around, it hits the same spot every few minutes. In the same way, the energy from a neutron star sweeps past Earth in a regular rhythm. Each time the stream of energy points toward Earth, astronomers can detect a pulse, or beat. The regular pulses led to the name pulsating stars, or pulsars for short.

The neutron star inside the Crab Nebula is a pulsar. As it spins, this pulsar's beam of energy seems to flash on and off. When its stream of energy points toward Earth, astronomers can detect the pulsar. When the stream of energy points away from Earth, astronomers can't find the pulsar.

This illustration of a neutron star shows its magnetic field in dark purple. The pink sections show radiation streaming away from the star at its north and south poles.

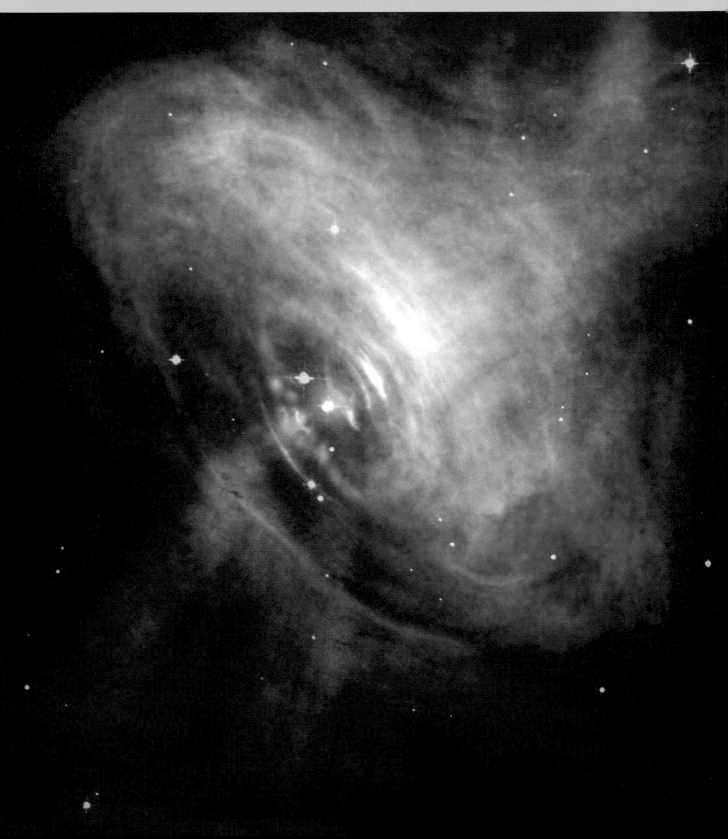

A pulsar inside the Crab Nebula flashes thirty times a second, sending out beams of light energy.

Many pulsars send out their stream of energy as radio waves. Radio waves are invisible. A few pulsars send out their beams of energy as visible light. The pulsar in the Crab Nebula is one of these. Its light flashes on and off thirty times a second.

The pulsar in the Crab Nebula has been sending regular signals for about a thousand years. Over the next two thousand years, its spinning will probably slow down. Its signals will grow weaker. If the signals grow very weak, people will no longer be able to detect them. After millions of years, the pulsar's signals will probably stop completely.

TUNING IN TO OUTER SPACE

Astronomers first discovered pulsars in 1967. Since then, astronomers have found thousands of pulsars. Astronomers often use radio telescopes to find pulsars' signals. Radio telescopes are not the kind of telescopes that people look through. Instead, radio telescopes collect radio waves from space. Once the waves are collected, astronomers can analyze them. With the help of radio telescopes, astronomers can "see" radio pulsars.

LITTLE GREEN *Men?*

In 1967 British astronomer Jocelyn Bell *(below left)* was studying space with a radio telescope. She noticed radio signals coming from an unknown object in space. These signals came regularly, every 1.3 seconds. What could be making these strange, regular signals? Could it be aliens from another planet? Bell gave the strange signals the nickname Little Green Men. She didn't really think aliens were making the signals. The name was mostly a joke.

To figure out what was making the regular signals, Bell worked with her teacher, British astronomer Anthony Hewish *(below right)*. After lots of work, Bell and Hewish realized that the strange, regular signals were coming from neutron stars. Later on, astronomers named the signaling stars pulsating stars, or pulsars.

The Arecibo Radio Telescope in Puerto Rico collects radio waves coming from pulsars and other objects in space.

   The largest radio telescope in the world is in Puerto Rico, an island in the Caribbean Sea. It is the Arecibo Radio Telescope, named for a nearby town. Astronomers often use this telescope to find pulsars. The telescope has a huge dish on top. Radio waves coming from space hit the inside of the dish. The dish sends the waves to an antenna. The antenna converts the waves to electrical signals. Astronomers study the signals using computers. The Arecibo Radio Telescope weighs about 600 tons (546 metric tons). Its dish is 1,000 feet (305 m) across.

Black Holes

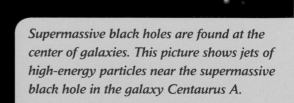

Supermassive black holes are found at the center of galaxies. This picture shows jets of high-energy particles near the supermassive black hole in the galaxy Centaurus A.

$\mathcal{B}$LACK HOLES ARE AN AMAZING WONDER IN THE UNIVERSE. THEY SEEM LIKE SOMETHING OUT OF A SCIENCE-FICTION MOVIE. BLACK HOLES ARE SO DENSE THAT NOTHING ESCAPES THE PULL OF THEIR IMMENSE GRAVITY. WHAT'S MORE, THESE OBJECTS ARE INVISIBLE. LIGHT GETS PULLED INTO BLACK HOLES AND TRAPPED INSIDE. THE LIGHT CAN'T ESCAPE FROM A BLACK HOLE, SO WE HAVE NO LIGHT TO SEE THEM BY. EVERYTHING THAT GETS TOO CLOSE TO A BLACK HOLE IS PULLED IN BY ITS GRAVITY AND THEN CRUSHED ALMOST OUT OF EXISTENCE.

This image shows a galaxy called NGC 4261. It contains dozens of black holes (the collapsed cores of supergiant stars from which nothing can escape). Although black holes are invisible, astronomers can find them using telescopes that detect X-rays. An X-ray telescope produced this image.

Black holes sound like science fiction, but scientists say they do exist. In fact, scientists have found lots of them. Some black holes are right in our own galaxy.

STELLAR BLACK HOLES

Astronomers have found two different types of black holes. One type is called a low-mass or stellar black hole. This kind of black hole forms when a supergiant star explodes in a supernova.

Every supergiant star will explode at the end of its life. When the star explodes, its outer layers will blow out into space. At the same time, its core will collapse. At this point, one of two things can happen to the core.

If the core has less than three times the mass of the Sun, it will collapse into a tiny ball of neutrons. It will become a tiny, dense neutron star.

If the core has more than three times the mass of the Sun, it will also collapse into a tiny ball of neutrons. But it won't stop there. The core will continue collapsing. Its own gravity will crush it into a single, extremely tiny point called a singularity. The singularity has a huge amount of gravity, yet it has no volume. Once the core is crushed down into a singularity, it ceases to exist as a core. Instead, it has become a stellar black hole.

The gravity of the black hole is unbelievably strong. Anything that comes too close to the black hole cannot escape from its pull. Even light can't escape. Since everything close by gets pulled in and nothing comes out, it truly is a hole in space. And since not even light can come out, it is a black hole.

"Supernovas give rise to some of the most bizarre objects in the universe—neutron stars and black holes."

—Alex Filippenko, U.S. astronomer, 2008

SUPERMASSIVE BLACK HOLES: AMAZING MONSTERS

The second kind of black hole is a supermassive black hole. As the name suggests, these black holes have a huge amount of mass. In fact, they have millions or even billions of times more mass than the Sun.

Supermassive black holes are found in the center of galaxies. In fact, our own Milky Way galaxy has a supermassive black hole at its center. Astronomers think these supermassive black holes form when several stars collapse. The collapsed stars might start out as individual stellar black holes. Then the individual black holes pull at one another until they merge into one enormous supermassive black hole.

An artist created this picture of a supermassive black hole at the center of a galaxy.

After a supermassive black hole forms, its incredible gravity sucks gas and dust from the surrounding area. At first the gas and dust swirl around the outside of the black hole. As they swirl, they become extremely hot and start to glow. The hot, glowing gas and dust give off X-rays and other forms of energy. As the gas and dust spin faster and faster, they are drawn in toward the boundary of the black hole itself. Once the gas and dust reach this boundary, they get pulled inside, at the speed of light, and crushed. Once inside the black hole, the squashed dust and gas cannot escape. Nothing can escape from a black hole—not even light.

Astronomers are studying supermassive black holes to learn more about them. In particular, they are studying the monster black hole in the middle of our galaxy. This black hole is named Sagittarius A* (pronounced Sagittarius A star). It got this name because it's located in a part of the galaxy called the Sagittarius Arm.

The event horizon is the point of no return for something approaching a black hole. Once beyond the horizon, there is no chance of escape.

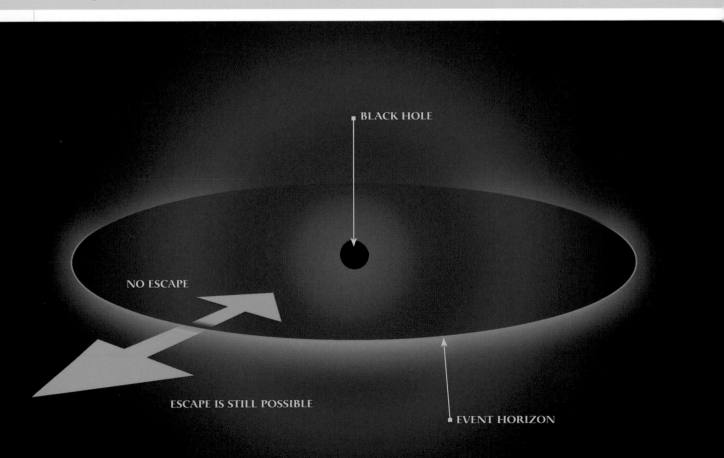

BLACK HOLE

NO ESCAPE

ESCAPE IS STILL POSSIBLE

EVENT HORIZON

> *"The stars do not stay still. And they do not always behave themselves! Some twinkle, and some explode. Some collapse, and some collide with other stars. Some even swallow up light."*
>
> —*Isaac Asimov, U.S. scientist, 1988*

HOW TO FIND A BLACK HOLE

If black holes are invisible, how can we study them—or even find them? Astronomers can't see black holes, even with the most powerful telescope.

Uhuru *is shown here in preflight tests at Goddard Space Flight Center in Maryland in 1970.*

How do you find something that is invisible? Astronomers look for black holes indirectly. If it seems like an immense amount of gravity is pulling at nearby stars and other objects but nothing visible is the source of that gravity, then astronomers know that a black hole might be lurking nearby.

In 1970 NASA launched a satellite named *Uhuru.* (The word *uhuru* means "freedom" in Swahili, a language of eastern Africa.) This satellite searched for objects in space that gave off powerful X-rays. *Uhuru* detected a lot of X-rays that seemed to come from a star in the constellation Cygnus. The star was a blue supergiant. Then astronomers noticed

This illustration shows the double star Cygnus X-1. The black hole in Cygnus X-1 pulls gases away from the blue supergiant star nearby.

that something invisible was pulling gases away from the blue star. This invisible something was pulling extremely hard and giving off lots of X-rays. The astronomers knew that only one thing could have so much gravitational pull and yet be invisible. It had to be a black hole!

The astronomers named this double star (the black hole and its neighboring blue star) Cygnus X-1. The black hole in Cygnus X-1 was the first one ever found. Since that discovery, astronomers have found many more black holes. They have found these black holes indirectly—by observing the way the black holes pull at other objects.

FROM DARK STAR *to Black Hole*

U.S. scientist John Wheeler came up with the term *black hole* in 1967, before people had actually found a black hole. Before that, astronomers used the name *dark stars* to describe the phenomenon.

Our own galaxy, the Milky Way, has a supermassive black hole at its center. The Chandra X-ray Observatory took this picture of red lobes of gas surrounding the black hole.

TIMELINE

1006   Observers in Egypt, Europe, and Asia report a bright new star in the sky. Modern astronomers determine that the "star" was really a supernova.

1054   Chinese astronomers spot a bright new "guest star," or supernova.

1572   Tycho Brahe makes the first detailed observations of a supernova.

1611   Galileo Galilei discovers sunspots on the Sun.

1868   Joseph Norman Lockyer identifies helium gas in the outer layer of the Sun.

1967   Jocelyn Bell discovers radio signals from the first known pulsar.

1971   Astronomers find the first known black hole in the double star Cygnus X-1.

1987   Ian Shelton discovers Supernova 1987A.

1995   NASA and ESA launched the spacecraft *SOHO*. This spacecraft monitors the Sun for solar activity and storms.

2003   NASA launches the Spitzer Space Telescope, which is used to study nebulas.

2006   NASA launches two *STEREO* spacecraft. These spacecraft track the Sun's stormy weather and take 3-D images of solar storms.

2010   NASA launches the *SDO* spacecraft. *SDO* collects information on solar storms and the Sun's magnetic field.

CHOOSE AN EIGHTH WONDER

Now that you've read *Seven Wonders of the Sun and Other Stars,* do a little research to choose an eighth wonder. You may enjoy working with a friend.

To start your research, look at some of the websites and books listed on the following pages. Use the Internet and library books to find more information. What other aspects of the Sun and stars are wondrous? Think about things that

- *Have been newly discovered*
- *Are still mysteries to astronomers*
- *Are extremely large or extremely small*

You might even try gathering photos and writing your own chapter on the eighth wonder.

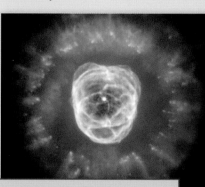

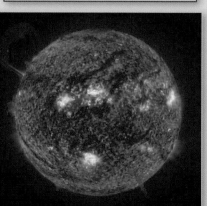

GLOSSARY

atmosphere: a blanket of gases that surrounds a planet or a star

aurora: a swirling display of colored lights in the sky, usually seen near the North Pole or the South Pole

black hole: an invisible place in space where gravity is so strong that nothing can escape from it. A black hole forms when the core of a massive star collapses.

constellation: a shape outlined or formed by stars in the sky

corona: the outermost layer of gases in the Sun's atmosphere

coronal mass ejection: a solar storm in which a gigantic blob of gas erupts from the Sun's corona

eclipse: the passing of one object in space in front of a second object, so that the light from the second object is blocked out. An example is the Moon blocking light from the Sun.

galaxy: a huge collection of stars, dust, and gas. Some galaxies, like our Milky Way, form giant spirals, while others have different shapes.

light-year: the distance that light travels in one year, about 5.88 trillion miles (9.46 trillion km)

magnetic field: the area around the Sun, Earth, or another object where magnetism can be felt. Magnetism is a force that pulls objects together or pushes them away from one another.

mass: the amount of material or matter in an object

nebula: an enormous cloud of gas and dust where new stars may begin to form

neutron star: the collapsed core of a large star, which is small and very dense

orbit: the path an object follows when it travels around another object. An example is Earth's path around the Sun.

pulsar: short for *pulsating star*; a neutron star that spins around and gives off regular signals or pulses

radiation: a kind of energy. Radiation includes radio waves, visible light, infrared rays, and X-rays, as well as other forms of energy.

solar eclipse: when the Moon passing in front of the Sun blocks the Sun's light

solar flare: a solar storm in which a sudden, violent explosion of burning gases blasts out from the Sun

solar prominence: a solar storm in which a dense tongue of burning gases loops out from the surface of the Sun into its atmosphere

solar system: the Sun and all the objects that travel around it

solar wind: a constant stream of radiation and particles flowing from the Sun

star: a gigantic ball of hot, burning gases

sunspots: dark, circular areas on the Sun's surface where solar storms occur

supergiant stars: the largest stars in the universe

supernova: explosions of certain types of stars. A Type II supernova occurs when a supergiant star blows up. A Type 1a supernova occurs when a white dwarf star blows up.

white dwarf: a dense planet-sized star created by the collapse of a small or medium-sized star

SOURCE NOTES

9   Lee Hansen, unpublished memoirs, Tuckahoe, New York, 2008.

11   Ken Croswell, *Ten Worlds* (Honesdale, PA: Boyds Mills Press, 2007), 6.

25   Fred Schaaf, *The 50 Best Sights in Astronomy and How to See Them* (Hoboken, NJ: John Wiley, 2007), 18.

27   Fred Whipple, *Orbiting the Sun* (Cambridge, MA: Harvard University Press, 1981), 105.

33   Mark Voit, *Hubble Space Telescope: New Views of the Universe* (New York: Harry N. Abrams, 2000), 24.

34   Henry Beston, *The Outermost House* (1928; repr., New York: Owl Books, 1992), 79.

38   Galileo Galilei, *Sidereus Nuncius* (Venice: Thomas Baglioni, 1610. Barker, Peter, editor. *Sidereus Nuncius*: Oklahoma City: Byzantium Press, 2004), 16b.

42   Ken Croswell, *The Lives of Stars* (Honesdale, PA: Boyds Mills Press, 2009) 34.

47   Alan Dyer, *Space* (Pleasantville, NY: Reader's Digest Children's Books, 1999), 52.

48   Gabrielle Walker and Robert Burnham. *Astronomy* (Pleasantville, NY: Reader's Digest, 1998), 40.

57   Ellen Jackson, *The Mysterious Universe* (Boston: Houghton Mifflin, 2008), 22.

58   David Aguilar, *Planets, Stars, and Galaxies* (Washington, DC: National Geographic, 2007), 107.

64   Jackson, *Mysterious Universe*, 52.

67   Isaac Asimov, *Isaac Asimov's Library of the Universe: Quasars, Pulsars, and Black Holes* (New York: Dell Yearling, 1988), 4.

SELECTED BIBLIOGRAPHY

Bennett, Jeffrey, Megan Donahue, Nicholas Schneider, and Mark Voit. *The Cosmic Perspective*. 5th ed. New York: Learning Solutions, 2009.

Espenak, Fred, Mark Littmann, and Ken Willcox. *Totality: Eclipses of the Sun*. New York: Oxford University Press, 1999.

Ferris, Timothy. *Seeing in the Dark*. New York: Simon and Schuster, 2002.

Glover, Linda K, comp. *National Geographic Encyclopedia of Space*. Washington, DC: National Geographic Society, 2005.

Schaff, Fred. *The 50 Best Sights in Astronomy and How to See Them*. Hoboken, NJ: John Wiley, 2007.

Zeilik, Michael. *Astronomy: The Evolving Universe*. New York: Cambridge University Press, 2002.

FURTHER READING AND WEBSITES

Books

Branley, Franklyn M. *Superstar: The Supernova of 1987*. New York: Thomas Y. Crowell, 1990. Branley gives a detailed account of the famous supernova of 1987. He also explains the science of supergiant stars and supernova explosions.

Croswell, Ken. *The Lives of Stars*. Honesdale, PA: Boyds Mills Press, 2009. Astronomer Ken Croswell leads a tour of stars: how they are born, age, and die. The book includes many large-format photographs.

Fleisher, Paul. *The Big Bang*. Minneapolis: Twenty-First Century Books, 2006. Fleisher explains the science behind the Big Bang theory and other mysteries of the universe.

Jackson, Ellen. *The Mysterious Universe*. Boston: Houghton Mifflin, 2008. This book discusses supernovas, dark energy, and black holes. The author also profiles astronomer Alex Filippenko and his fellow scientists.

Landau, Elaine. *The Sun*. New York: Children's Press, 2008. Landau's introduction to the Sun offers a lively, fact-filled overview of this topic.

Miller, Ron. *Satellites*. Minneapolis: Twenty-First Century Books, 2008. Learn about the innovations and history of satellite technology.

Silverstein, Alvin, Virginia Silverstein, and Laura Silverstein Nunn. *The Universe*. Minneapolis: Twenty-First Century Books, 2009. This well-regarded overview of the universe for young readers has recently been fully revised and updated.

Simon, Seymour. *Stars*. New York: Collins, 2006. Well-known author Simon provides a clear, helpful overview of stars: their composition and life cycles. The book includes many interesting photos.

Thomson, Sarah L. *Extreme Stars! Q & A*. New York: HarperCollins, 2006. In this book, author Thomson offers a short and lively introduction to stars, supernovas, black holes, the death of stars, and more.

Vogt, Gregory L. *Earth's Outer Atmosphere*. Minneapolis: Twenty-First Century Books, 2007. Learn about Earth's outer atmosphere, the transition zone between the planet and outer space—the place where Earth first interacts with the Sun's energy.

World Book. *The Sun and Other Stars*. Chicago: World Book, 2007. World Book's introduction to the Sun and other stars offers basic information on these topics.

Websites

Ask an Astrophysicist

http://imagine.gsfc.nasa.gov/docs/ask_astro/ask_an_astronomer.html
This website from NASA has clear, detailed answers to frequently asked questions about stars, supernovas, black holes, and related topics.

Astronomy for Kids

http://frontiernet.net/~kidpower/astronomy.html
This site gives information on stars, galaxies, the solar system, and more.

Imagine the Universe

http://imagine.gsfc.nasa.gov/docs/science/science.html
At this website from NASA, you can find detailed information on stars, black holes, neutron stars, supernovas, and related space topics.

Solar Eclipses: 2011–2020

http://eclipse.gsfc.nasa.gov/SEdecade/SEdecade2011.html
This NASA website has detailed information on solar eclipses of all types (total, annular, and partial) from the years 2011 to 2020.

Space Weather Center

http://www.spaceweathercenter.org
This website has lots of interesting information on the Sun, solar storms, and auroras.

Star Child

http://starchild.gsfc.nasa.gov/docs/StarChild/StarChild.html
Visit this NASA website to find a variety of information on stars, planets, and the wonders of the universe.

INDEX

ABOUT THE AUTHOR

Rosanna Hansen has worked as a children's book publisher, editor, and author. Most recently, she served as publisher and editor-in-chief of *Weekly Reader*, where she supervised the publication of seventeen classroom magazines as well as books. Before that, she was group publisher of Reader's Digest Children's Books for the United States and the United Kingdom.

Hansen has written more than twenty children's books on such topics as astronomy, nature, and animals. In her free time, she enjoys stargazing and volunteers with wildlife organizations. She and her husband, Corwith, live in Tuckahoe, New York.

PHOTO ACKNOWLEDGMENTS

The images in this book are used with the permission of: © Frank Zullo/Photo Researchers, Inc., p. 5; © Skylab/NRL/Roger Ressmeyer/CORBIS, p. 6; SOHO (ESA & NASA), pp. 7; 12 (bottom); © Daryl Pederson/Alaskastock/Photolibrary, p. 9; NASA/JPL, pp. 10, 71 (middle/bottom); © Laura Westlund/Independent Picture Service, pp. 12 (top), 21, 26, 30; © American Institute of Physics, p. 13; © The Print Collector/Photolibrary, p. 14; National Optical Astronomy Observatory/Association of Universities for Research in Astronomy/National Science Foundation (NOAO), p. 15; NASA/Goddard/SOHO Project Office, p. 16; NASA/MSFC/Janet Salverson, p. 17; © Westend61/SuperStock, p. 18; © Bridgeman-Giraudon/Art Resource, NY, p. 19; © Siegfried Layda/Photographer's Choice/Getty Images, p. 20; © John W. Bova/Photo Researchers, Inc., p. 22; © Atlas Photo Bank/Photo Researchers, Inc., p. 24 (top); © ChinaFoto Press/Getty Images, p. 24 (bottom); © Photo by Hulton Archive/Getty Images, pp. 25, 52; © Rev. Ronald Royer/Photo Researchers, Inc., p. 27; NASA, ESA, The Hubble Heritage Team (STScI/AURA), M. Robberto (Space Telescope Science Institute) and the Hubble Space Telescope Orion Treasury Project Team, pp. 28, 71 (top/right); NASA/JPL-Caltech, pp. 29, 65, 71 (top/left); NASA, H. Ford (JHU), G. Illingworth (UCSC/LO), M.Clampin (STScI), G. Hartig (STScI), the ACS Science Team, and ESA, p. 31; © European Southern Observatory/Photo Researchers, Inc., pp. 32 (top), 45; © Robert Gendler/Visuals Unlimited, Inc., p. 32 (bottom); NASA/ESA/Hubble SM4 ERO Team, p. 35; © Lee C. Coombs/Phototake Inc./Alamy, p. 36; NASA/STScI Digitized Sky Survey/Noel Carbonip, p. 37; © Yoji Hirose/Galaxy Picture Library/Alamy, p. 38; © Davide De Martin/Photo Researchers, Inc., p. 39; © Eckhard Slawik/Photo Researchers, Inc., p. 40; NASA, ESA, and The Hubble Heritage Team (STScI/AURA), pp. 43, 49; © Science Source/Photo Researchers, Inc., p. 44; © European Southern Observatory/Photo Researchers, Inc., pp. 32 (top), 45; NASA/CXC/SAO, pp. 47, 71 (bottom/left); © Malcolm Park/Oxford Scientific/Photolibrary, p. 50; © Mark Garlick/Photo Researchers, Inc., p. 51; NASA, ESA and H.E. Bond (STScI), pp. 53, 71 (middle/right); NASA/CXC/STScI/JPL-Caltech/UIUC/Univ. of Minn., p. 53; NASA/ESA/JPL/Arizona State Univ., p. 54; © Christian Darkin/Photo Researchers, Inc., p. 55; © Mark Garlick/Photo Researchers, Inc., p. 56; © Chris Butler/Photo Researchers, Inc., p. 58; NASA/CXC/HST/ASU/J. Hester et al., p. 59; © Brian Seed/Time & Life Pictures/Getty Images, p. 60; © David Parker/Photo Researchers, Inc., p. 61; NASA/CXC/CfA/R.Kraft et al, p. 62; NASA/CXC/A. Zezas et al., p. 63; © Ron Miller, p. 66; © Photo by SSPL/Getty Images, p. 67; © David A. Hardy, Futures: 50 years in Space/Photo Researchers, Inc, p. 68; NASA/CXC/MIT/F.K.Baganoff et al., p. 69; NASA, Andrew Fruchter and the ERO Team [Sylvia Baggett (STScI), Richard Hook (ST-ECF), Zoltan Levay (STScI)], p. 71 (top/middle); © Martin Bernetti/AFP/Getty Images, p. 71 (bottom/right).

Front Cover: © Martin Bernetti/AFP/Getty Images (top, right); NASA/JPL (top, middle); NASA/CXC/SAO (top/left); NASA, ESA and H.E. Bond (STScI) (middle); NASA, ESA, The Hubble Heritage Team (STScI/AURA), M. Robberto (Space Telescope Science Institute) and the Hubble Space Telescope Orion Treasury Project Team (bottom, left); NASA, Andrew Fruchter and the ERO Team [Sylvia Baggett (STScI), Richard Hook (ST-ECF), Zoltan Levay (STScI)], (bottom, middle);NASA/JPL-Caltech (bottom, right).